I0569104

Alchemy of the Heart

Turning Grief, Love, and Loss into Living Gold

by Joy Hafner
TrueJoy Publishing

COPYRIGHT PAGE

Alchemy of the Heart: Turning Grief, Love, and Loss into Living Gold

This book is published by:
TrueJoy Publishing
Author: Joy Hafner
Publisher: TrueJoy Publishing
ISBN: 978-1-971164-88-5
ISBN: 978-1-971164-89-2
Cover design by TrueJoy Publishing
Interior design by TrueJoy Publishing
Printed in the United States of America
First Edition

Book Intention (Internal Compass)

This book is not about fixing pain.
It is about **listening to it until it transforms**.

Alchemy of the Heart explores grief in all its forms—death, heartbreak, identity loss, lost dreams, endings that arrive without permission—and reveals how pain, when met with presence, becomes a sacred initiator.

This is a guide for those who have loved deeply, lost profoundly, and are ready to stop abandoning themselves in the aftermath.

A Letter to the Reader

Dear Reader,

If this book found its way into your hands, it is not by accident.

Something in you has loved deeply.
Something in you has lost.
And something in you is ready—not to bypass the pain, but to live honestly again.

I want you to know this from the beginning:
this book is not here to fix you.

You are not broken.

Alchemy of the Heart was written as a companion—not a prescription, not a timeline, not a set of answers to master. It is meant to be read slowly, out of order if needed, with pauses that matter more than progress.

There may be chapters you move through easily.
There may be others you need to sit with for days, weeks, or return to years later.

Please trust that rhythm.

This book does not ask you to relive what hurt you.
It asks you to **stay present with yourself** as you are now.

You will find moments that feel tender, grounding, clarifying, and at times uncomfortable. That does not mean you are doing it wrong. It means something true is touching the surface.

When emotions arise, pause.
When the body asks for rest, listen.
When you feel the urge to rush toward meaning, slow down
instead.

The Alchemy Pauses are not optional suggestions—they are
invitations back into yourself. Even one breath is enough.

There is no "right" way to grieve.
No correct speed for healing.
No finish line you are meant to cross.

What matters is not how quickly you move forward,
 but how gently you remain with yourself while you do.

If at any point this book feels like too much, close it.
If it feels like a mirror, take your time.
If it feels like relief, let that be okay too.

Joy is not a betrayal.
Rest is not avoidance.
Living fully is not a denial of love.

This work is not about letting go of what mattered.
It is about learning how to **carry it without losing yourself**.

Above all, let this book remind you of something you may have
forgotten:

You are allowed to be here exactly as you are.
You are allowed to take up space in your own life.
And you are allowed to become a safe place for yourself—again
and again.

May these pages meet you where you are.
May they walk beside you without asking you to hurry.
And may you discover, in your own time,
that the gold you were searching for
has been forming within you all along.

With tenderness and trust,
Joy
TrueJoy Publishing

Structure Overview

Part I — The Breaking

When the heart shatters, not to punish—but to open

Part II — The Fire

Where pain becomes the initiator

Part III — The Alchemy

The sacred turning

Part IV — The Gold

Living after loss—not smaller, but truer

Ritual Threads (woven throughout)

- Heart-centered reflections
- Simple alchemy rituals (water, fire, breath, writing)
- Somatic check-ins
- "If you're here, try this" moments
- Gentle pauses instead of prescriptions

Opening Pages

Prologue — The Heart Knows Before We Do

Grief does not arrive as a lesson.
It arrives as a rupture.

A sudden tearing of the fabric that once held your life
together— the version of you who believed love was permanent,
that plans would unfold, that endings would be negotiated
gently.

But grief does not ask for permission.
It does not explain itself.
It simply opens you.

This book was born not from answers,
but from sitting on the floor of my own life
when everything familiar fell away and discovering that
something ancient remained.

Not strength.
Not positivity.
Presence.

What I learned is this:
The heart is not fragile.
It is **alchemical**.

It breaks only to widen.
It burns only to purify.
And when we stop trying to escape the fire,
it reveals a quieter, steadier gold.

Part I — The Breaking

When the heart shatters, not to punish—but to open

Chapter One — The Moment Everything Changed

There is always a before.

Before the loss had a name.
Before the body understood what the mind could not yet hold.
Before the moment your life split into two timelines—
the one you lived in unconsciously,
and the one you were initiated into without consent.

Grief rarely announces itself.
It slips in sideways.

A sentence spoken too quickly.
A silence that lasts too long.
A feeling in the chest that doesn't move when everything else does.

And suddenly, the life you were standing inside of no longer fits.

The world keeps going—emails arrive, the sun rises, people ask what you need—but something fundamental has shifted. You are still here, yet the version of you who believed things were stable has quietly dissolved.

This is not weakness. This is awakening through rupture.

The Shock of the After

Most people think grief is sadness.

But the first thing grief takes is **orientation**.

Time bends.
Your body moves slower or faster than you expect.
Simple decisions feel strangely heavy.
You forget what you were saying mid-sentence—not because you are broken, but because your nervous system has entered unfamiliar territory.

Grief pulls you out of the mind and drops you into the body without instructions.

This is why advice feels hollow in the beginning.
Why platitudes land like static.
Why "being strong" feels exhausting instead of empowering.

The heart has lost a structure it relied on.

And structures do not collapse quietly.

What Was Really Lost

We often name grief by its surface loss:
a person, a relationship, a role, a dream.

But beneath every loss is something subtler.

A future you were already living toward.
A version of yourself you hadn't finished becoming.
A sense of safety you didn't realize you were borrowing.

Grief is not only the absence of what was.
It is the sudden removal of what *might have been*.

And no one teaches us how to mourn futures.

So we minimize.
We rush.
We tell ourselves it "could have been worse."

But the heart does not operate on comparison.
It operates on attachment and meaning.

And meaning does not disappear just because the world
thinks it should.

The Spiritual Urge to Escape

If you are someone who has walked a spiritual path, grief can feel especially confusing.

You may tell yourself:

- Everything happens for a reason.
- Love never dies.
- This is part of my growth.

And while these things may eventually hold truth, they can become armor when used too soon.

Grief does not want to be transcended.
 It wants to be **met**.

Spiritual bypassing is not a moral failure—it is a survival response.
A way the psyche tries to regain control when the heart has lost it.

But grief is not asking for enlightenment.
It is asking for presence.

The kind that sits on the floor with it.
The kind that breathes when answers don't come.
The kind that stays.

The Invitation Hidden Inside the Pain

Here is what most people are never told:

Grief is not here to destroy you.
It is here to **introduce you to a deeper truth of yourself.**

Not the polished self.
Not the capable self.
Not the one who knows how to hold it together.

But the self beneath performance.
The one who loves without guarantees.
The one who can feel without collapsing.
The one who learns, slowly, how to remain open even
when life has proven impermanent.

This is not resilience as endurance. This is resilience as
intimacy with reality. Grief strips away illusion—not to
punish, but to clarify.

Alchemy Pause — The Ground

Feel the surface beneath you.

The chair.
The floor.
The earth holding you without effort.

You are supported, even here.

Let that land.

A Gentle Reframe

What if the question is not
"How do I get through this?"

What if the question is
"How do I stay with myself while this moves through
me?"

Grief does not need to be rushed into meaning.
Meaning arrives organically when grief is allowed to
breathe.

Your only task in the beginning is this:

Do not abandon yourself.

Stay close.
Listen without fixing.
Let the heart speak in its own language—through tears,
numbness, anger, exhaustion, longing.

This is not the end of your life.

This is the end of an orientation that could no longer hold
who you are becoming.

Closing Reflection

If you are here, reading these words, something in you
already knows:

You are not broken.
You are opened.

And while this opening may feel unbearable at times,
it is also the doorway through which a truer, quieter, more
sovereign love will eventually emerge.

Not today.
Not on command.

But in its own time.

Pause (No Fixing Required)

Place one hand on your chest.
Notice the temperature beneath your palm.
Notice the rhythm of your breath.

You do not need to name what hurts yet.
You do not need to understand it.

Just acknowledge this truth:

I am here. And that is enough for now.

Chapter Two — Grief Is Not a Problem to Solve

Most of us meet grief the way we were taught to meet discomfort: with urgency.

We ask questions like *How long will this last?*
What should I be doing?
What's the lesson?

We search for timelines.
We look for experts.
We gather advice as if grief were a riddle that could be cracked with enough effort.

But grief does not respond to strategy.

Grief responds to **presence**.

It is not a malfunction in the system.
It is the system responding honestly to love and loss.

When we treat grief like a problem, we subtly communicate to ourselves that something has gone wrong—that our sadness is excessive, our anger inconvenient, our numbness suspicious. We begin to monitor ourselves, manage our emotions, and measure our healing against an invisible standard.

This is where grief quietly turns into suffering.

The Fix-It Reflex

The mind wants resolution.
It wants meaning it can file away and move past.

So it says:

- *Stay busy.*

- *Be grateful.*

- *Focus on the positive.*

- *Everything happens for a reason.*

These phrases are not inherently wrong.
They are simply mistimed.

They arrive before the body has finished speaking.

Grief lives first in sensation, not insight.
In the tightening of the chest.
The heaviness behind the eyes.
The fatigue that sleep does not touch.

When we rush to understand grief, we skip the essential step of **feeling it**. And what is unfelt does not disappear—it waits.

Often in the body.
Often in patterns.
Often in the places we least expect.

What Grief Actually Is

Grief is love encountering impermanence.

That's it.

It is not a sign of weakness.
It is evidence of depth.

If you are grieving deeply, it means you loved deeply.
If you feel undone, it means something meaningful passed
through your life.

The pain is not the enemy.
The resistance to pain is.

Grief only becomes overwhelming when it is denied,
minimized, or forced to hurry.

Left alone—met gently, consistently—it moves like
weather.
It has seasons.
It has pauses.
It has moments of quiet that surprise you.

The Permission You Were Never Given

No one teaches us how to *be* with grief.

We are taught how to endure it.
How to distract from it.
How to turn it into productivity or wisdom as quickly as
possible.

But grief does not need to be earned away.

You are allowed to be sad without explanation.
You are allowed to miss what hurt you.
You are allowed to feel both relieved and devastated.
You are allowed to take longer than others are comfortable
with.

Grief does not ask for efficiency.
It asks for honesty.

Letting Grief Be What It Is

When you stop trying to solve grief, something subtle
shifts.

The body exhales.
The nervous system softens.
The heart feels less alone.

You realize you don't need to *do* anything with grief today.

You only need to **stay in relationship with yourself** while it moves.

This is where alchemy begins—not in transformation, but in allowance.

Alchemy Pause — The Breath

Pause here.

Before continuing, take a slow breath in through your nose.
Let it fill you gently.

Now exhale through your mouth,
just a little longer than the inhale.

Again.
Inhale—no rush.
Exhale—letting the shoulders drop, the jaw soften.

You are not trying to calm yourself.
You are letting your body know it doesn't have to be fixed.

Stay for three breaths.

When you're ready, remind yourself quietly:

I am allowed to feel this without solving it.

A New Orientation

What if healing is not about getting somewhere else?

What if it is about **learning how to stay present where you are—**
without self-judgment, without timelines, without comparison?

Grief does not need to be carried perfectly.
It only needs to be carried *truthfully*.

You don't have to make meaning yet.
You don't have to be brave today.

You only have to keep yourself company.

That is not avoidance.
That is devotion.

Closing Reflection

Grief is not asking to be solved.
It is asking to be respected.

When you stop treating it like a problem,
it begins to reveal itself as a passage.

One that changes you—
not by force,
but by intimacy.

Alchemy Pause — Closing

Before turning the page, take one final breath.

Notice what feels even slightly different than when you began—
not better, not worse—just different.

Let that be enough for now.

Continue when you're ready.

Chapter Three — Love That Had No Place to Land

One of the most confusing aspects of grief is not the pain.
It is the **love**.

The love that didn't disappear when the person left.
The love that still rises in your chest with nowhere to go.
The love that feels too big, too present, too alive for an
ending that already happened.

No one warns you about this part.

We expect grief to feel like absence.
But often, it feels like **overflow**.

You wake up and your heart still reaches.
You think of them without trying.
You feel tenderness arrive before logic can stop it.

And then comes the quiet question:
What am I supposed to do with all this love now?

When Love Outlives Its Form

We are taught that love needs an object.
A person.
A role.
A future.

So when the form disappears, we assume love should follow.

But love does not obey structure.
It is not loyal to timelines or outcomes.
It does not exit just because something ended.

Love is an energy that continues long after the relationship, the body, or the dream has changed shape.

This is why grief hurts the way it does.

It is not just loss.
It is love still alive in a world that no longer knows where to place it.

The Shame Around Lingering Love

Many people carry quiet shame about this.

They think:

- *I should be over this by now.*

- *Why do I still miss them?*

- *Does this mean I'm stuck?*

But lingering love is not failure.
It is evidence of depth and sincerity.

The heart does not unsubscribe just because the mind understands what happened.

And when we judge ourselves for still loving, we create a second wound—
not from loss, but from **self-rejection**.

Grief becomes heavier when love is made wrong.

Love Without a Destination

Here is something rarely spoken:

Love does not need to go somewhere to be valid.

It does not need to be reciprocated.
It does not need to be witnessed.
It does not need to be productive.

Sometimes love simply needs to be **felt**.

When you allow love to exist without demanding a destination, something softens. The ache becomes less sharp. The longing less frantic.

Love begins to change from something you are holding too tightly
into something that is holding *you*.

This is not detachment.
It is maturation.

The Ache Beneath the Ache

Often what hurts most is not just missing someone.

It is missing:

- who you were when you loved them

- the way your heart opened

- the version of yourself that felt seen, chosen, alive

Grief is not only about another person.

It is about the parts of *you* that came alive in their presence—and now wonder if they will ever have a place to exist again.

This is why grief feels personal.

It is personal.

Alchemy Pause — The Heart

Pause here.

Place one hand gently over your heart.

Notice if there is warmth, tightness, ache, or nothing at all.
There is no correct experience.

Instead of asking *why* you feel this, try simply noticing *that* you
feel it.

Let the feeling exist without explanation.

If it feels right, silently offer yourself this truth:

The love I feel is not a mistake.

Stay for a few breaths.

Letting Love Breathe

When love has no place to land, it can feel suffocating.

But when love is allowed to breathe—
without urgency, without interpretation—
it slowly reorganizes itself. It becomes less about grasping
and more about presence.

Less about longing and more about remembrance. Love
does not disappear. It transforms. Not because you force it
to— but because you finally stop trying to control it.

A New Way of Holding Love

What if love is not something to resolve,
but something to **integrate**?

What if the love you still feel is teaching you how deeply
you are capable of opening—
and how much of that capacity belongs to *you*, not the one
who left?

Love does not leave you empty. It leaves you expanded.
And expansion, at first, can feel unbearably tender.

Closing Reflection

If your heart still loves,
it is not because you are stuck.

It is because you are human.

You are allowed to carry love forward—
not as attachment,
but as wisdom.

Not as ache, but as proof of your depth.

Alchemy Pause — Closing

Before continuing, take one gentle breath into your heart.

Imagine creating just a little more space around the feeling—
not to push it away,
but to let it rest.

Continue when you feel ready.

Chapter Four — The Myth of "Moving On"

One of the first questions grief encounters is also one of the most damaging:

Have you moved on yet?

It arrives disguised as concern.
As encouragement.
As hope.

But beneath it lives an assumption—that healing has a finish line, that grief expires, that love should know when to stop speaking.

We are taught to believe that *moving on* is the goal.

But grief does not move on.

It **moves through**.

And only when allowed to move through does it change shape.

Where the Myth Came From

Our culture is uncomfortable with anything that cannot be optimized.

We like progress we can measure.
Emotions we can regulate quickly.
Pain that performs improvement on schedule.

So we invented a narrative:
Grief is something you pass through, graduate from, and leave behind.

But the heart does not heal by forgetting.
It heals by **integrating**.

And integration does not look like erasure.

What "Moving On" Often Really Means

For many people, moving on becomes a form of self-protection.

It means:

- suppressing tenderness before it becomes visible
- avoiding memories that still carry charge
- rushing into new roles, relationships, or identities
- replacing presence with distraction

This is not wrong.

It is human.

But when moving on is used to bypass grief rather than honor it, something essential remains unfinished.

The body remembers what the mind avoids.

And grief that is hurried does not disappear—
it becomes quieter, heavier, and more embedded.

The Difference Between Stuck and Loyal

There is an important distinction rarely made:

Being *stuck* means you cannot access life.

Being *loyal* means you refuse to pretend that what mattered didn't.

Grief often looks like stagnation from the outside
when it is actually **devotion** on the inside.

You are not stuck because you still feel.
You are not failing because love still arrives unannounced.

You are honoring something real.

The problem is not grief.

The problem is the demand that grief conform to someone else's comfort.

What Healing Actually Looks Like

Healing is not the absence of sadness.

It is the **expansion of capacity**.

You may still miss them—but you laugh again.
You may still ache—but you rest more deeply.
You may still carry memory—but it no longer defines your nervous system.

Healing is when grief becomes part of your landscape, not the whole horizon.

You don't leave it behind.

You learn how to walk with it.

Alchemy Pause — The Question

Pause here.

Ask yourself—gently, without needing an answer:

What am I afraid would happen if I stopped trying to "move on"?

Let the question settle.

Notice what arises in the body before the mind responds.

There is no right insight here—only honesty.

Stay with it for a few breaths.

Release Without Erasure

Letting go does not mean letting go of love.

It means letting go of the idea that love must look the way it once did.

It means releasing the version of the future that required a specific outcome to feel safe.

Grief is not asking you to forget.

It is asking you to **update your relationship with what was**.

This is a subtler, braver form of release.

You Are Allowed to Carry What Matters

There is no expiration date on meaning.

You are allowed to remember.
You are allowed to feel tenderness years later.
You are allowed to let love visit without turning it into a setback.

The heart does not measure time the way calendars do.

It measures truth.

Closing Reflection

You do not need to move on from what shaped you.

You only need to stop running from it.

Healing is not a departure.

It is a deepening.

Alchemy Pause — Closing

Before turning the page, take one breath.

Imagine loosening your grip—not on love,
but on the expectation that healing should look a certain way.

Continue when you're ready.

Chapter Five — The Body Keeps the Ledger

Before the mind understands what has happened,
the body already knows.

It tightens.
It slows.
It braces.
It forgets how to rest.

Grief is not only an emotional experience—it is a
physiological one.
It imprints itself in muscle, breath, posture, appetite, sleep.
Long after the story has been told and retold, the body
continues to keep record.

Not to punish you.
Not because something is wrong.

But because the body's job is to remember what mattered.

Where Grief Lives

Grief often hides in places we don't think to look:

In the jaw that clenches when you are quiet.
In the chest that feels heavy without explanation.
In the fatigue that does not lift with rest.
In the gut that tightens around ordinary decisions.

The body does not speak in sentences.
It speaks in sensation.

And when we ignore those sensations—when we override them with productivity, positivity, or pressure—the body becomes louder.

Not dramatic.
Persistent.

Why Talking Isn't Always Enough

We are often encouraged to "process" grief by talking about it.

And words matter.
Witnessing matters.

But grief does not live solely in language.

Some experiences happen too quickly, too deeply, or too early to be organized into narrative. They bypass the thinking mind and settle directly into the nervous system.

This is why you can understand what happened
and still feel frozen.
Why you can explain the loss
and still feel breathless.

Insight does not automatically equal integration.

The body must be included.

The Nervous System After Loss

Loss signals danger to the body—even when it is
emotional.

The nervous system may respond by:

- staying on high alert

- shutting down sensation

- oscillating between numbness and overwhelm

This is not dysfunction.
It is adaptation.

Your body learned how to survive something that
exceeded its expectations of safety.

Grief becomes heavier when we interpret these responses
as personal failure instead of intelligence.

The body is not holding grief *against* you.

It is holding it *for* you—until you have the capacity to receive it gently.

~

Listening Instead of Forcing

Many people try to heal grief by pushing their body back into normal.

Back into routines.
Back into productivity.
Back into strength.

But the body does not heal through force.

It heals through **permission**.

Permission to slow.
Permission to feel without interpretation.
Permission to rest without justification.

When you stop asking the body to perform and start asking it to communicate, the relationship changes.

The body softens when it feels respected.

Alchemy Pause — The Body

Pause here.

Bring your attention to your body.

Without trying to change anything, notice:
Where do you feel this chapter right now?

Chest?
Throat?
Shoulders?
Belly?
Lower back?

Choose one place that is asking for attention.

Place a hand there if it feels supportive.

Do not analyze the sensation.
Do not name it correctly.

Simply acknowledge it.

Stay for three slow breaths.

Silently offer yourself this truth:

My body is allowed to take up space in this healing.

When the Body Begins to Trust Again

As the body feels safer, grief begins to move.

Not all at once.
Not dramatically.

Sometimes it shows up as a sigh.
A yawn.
A tear that surprises you.
A sudden wave of fatigue or relief.

These are not setbacks.

They are signs that something frozen is thawing.

The body releases grief in layers,
 at the pace of safety—not desire.

You Do Not Have to Relive to Release

There is a quiet fear many people carry:

If I let myself feel this in my body, I will fall apart.

But the body does not ask you to relive the past.

It asks you to **notice the present**.

Sensation moves when it is acknowledged—not when it is
forced into story.

You can heal without re-traumatizing yourself.

You can listen without drowning.

The body knows the difference.

Closing Reflection

Your body has been with you through every loss,
every adaptation,
every moment you survived quietly.

It is not behind in healing.

It has simply been waiting for you to listen.

Alchemy Pause — Closing

Before turning the page, take one breath
and feel the surface supporting you.

You are held—here, now, in this body.

Continue when you're ready.

Part II — The Fire

Where pain becomes the initiator

Chapter Six — Sitting in the Ashes

After the breaking, after the body begins to speak, there comes a quieter—often more difficult—phase.

Nothing dramatic is happening anymore.
The initial shock has passed.
The world expects forward motion.

But inside, you are standing in the aftermath.

This is the ash.

The place where what once burned brightly has collapsed into something unrecognizable.
The place where there are no clear emotions to perform—only a dull, persistent presence.

Many people mistake this phase for stagnation.

It is not.

It is **integration** beginning its slow work.

When the Fire Has Gone Quiet

Early grief can feel sharp and consuming.
But later grief often feels muted, heavy, and strangely empty.

You may notice:

- a lack of motivation without sadness

- a neutrality that feels unsettling

- a sense of waiting without knowing for what

This is not numbness as pathology.

This is the nervous system recalibrating after intensity.

Ash is what remains when something has fully burned.
It is not lifeless—it is rich, mineral, potent.

But it looks like nothing.

The Discomfort of Stillness

Ash asks something counterintuitive:

Do not rush to rebuild.

We are conditioned to respond to loss by constructing meaning, identity, or replacement as quickly as possible.

But when rebuilding begins too soon, it often recreates what already failed to hold us.

Ash is the pause between identities.
The space where old roles no longer fit and new ones have not yet formed.

It can feel disorienting because there is nothing to grasp.

This is where many people abandon themselves—out of boredom, fear, or pressure to be "better."

But ash does not need fixing.

It needs **presence**.

Why Sitting Matters

When you allow yourself to sit in the ashes, something subtle happens.

You stop performing grief.
You stop narrating healing.
You stop trying to make sense of what cannot yet be named.

In this stillness, your system learns a crucial truth:

I can remain here without disappearing.

This is the moment the nervous system begins to trust again.

Not because things are resolved,
but because you are no longer fleeing.

Alchemy Pause — The Ground (Deeper)

Pause here.

Feel the weight of your body.

Notice the places where you are being supported—
the chair beneath you,
the floor,
the earth holding you without effort.

Let your shoulders drop slightly.
Let your jaw soften.

You are not waiting for clarity.
You are allowing stability.

Stay for three breaths.

Silently remind yourself:

I do not have to rebuild yet.

Ash Is Not Emptiness

We confuse ash with absence.

But ash is **fertile**.

In nature, ash enriches soil.
It prepares the ground for what comes next.

In grief, ash performs the same function.

It dissolves illusion.
It clears false urgency.
It reveals what truly matters—because everything else has fallen away.

What remains is quieter, truer, and more essential.

Trusting the Unformed

One of the hardest parts of this phase is not knowing who you are becoming.

There is no vision yet.
No excitement to lean toward.
No promise you can articulate.

Just a sense that you are no longer who you were.

Ash teaches patience without reward.

It asks you to trust life before it looks appealing again. This is not passivity. This is **deep listening**.

What Emerges in the Ash

If you stay long enough—without forcing meaning—you may notice:

- clearer boundaries
- a lower tolerance for what is misaligned
- a quieter inner voice that feels more honest
- a deepened sensitivity to what nourishes you

These are not conclusions.

They are signals.

Life reorganizing itself around truth instead of survival.

Closing Reflection

You are not empty.

You are resting in what remains
after what was false has burned away.

Ash is not the end of the fire. It is the ground from which a more honest flame will rise.

Alchemy Pause — Closing

Before turning the page, take one breath
and feel the steadiness beneath you.

Nothing needs to happen next.

Continue when you're ready.

Chapter Seven — Anger, Guilt, and the Unspoken

There are emotions that receive permission in grief—
sadness, longing, tenderness.

And then there are the others.

Anger.
Resentment.
Relief.
Guilt for surviving.
Guilt for not missing them the way you think you should.
Guilt for missing them too much.

These emotions tend to arrive quietly,
then retreat the moment they feel judged.

So they stay underground.

Not gone.
Just unspoken.

The Anger No One Asked About

Anger often surprises people in grief.

You may feel angry at:

- the person who left
- the circumstances that changed everything
- yourself, for what you did or didn't do
- life, for not being fair or gentle

This anger does not mean you are ungrateful.
It does not cancel out love.

Anger is simply energy that had nowhere safe to go.

When grief strips away control, anger tries to restore it.

Not elegantly—
but honestly.

Guilt as a Companion Emotion

Where anger exists, guilt is rarely far behind.

Guilt for feeling angry.
Guilt for moments of relief.
Guilt for laughter returning too soon—or too late.
Guilt for being here when someone else is not.

Guilt convinces you that pain must be performed perfectly
to be valid.

But grief is not a moral exam.

There is no correct emotional order.
No hierarchy of acceptable feelings.

The heart holds contradiction naturally—
 only the mind insists on purity.

The Cost of Silence

When anger and guilt are not acknowledged, they don't
disappear.

They turn inward.

They become self-criticism.
Chronic tension.
Fatigue without explanation.
A quiet sense of being "off" around others.

Unexpressed emotion does not stay neutral.
It calcifies.

Not because you failed—
but because it never felt safe to speak.

Letting the Unspoken Exist

Healing does not require dramatic release.

It requires **permission**.

Permission to admit what you feel without justifying it.
Permission to feel emotions that do not match your values.
Permission to experience grief as layered, not linear.

Anger does not need to be acted out.
Guilt does not need to be indulged.

They need to be **witnessed**.

The moment an emotion is allowed to exist,
it begins to soften.

Alchemy Pause — The Breath (Release Focus)

Pause here.

Take a slow inhale through your nose.

As you exhale through your mouth,
imagine releasing pressure from the jaw, the shoulders, the chest.

Again.

Let the exhale be audible if it wants to be.

You are not forcing emotion out.
You are creating space for it to move safely.

Stay for three breaths.

Silently remind yourself:

I am allowed to feel what I feel.

Anger as Information

Anger often carries clarity.

It points to violated boundaries.
Unmet needs.
Truths that were swallowed to keep peace.

When you listen to anger without letting it drive, it becomes instructive instead of destructive.

It shows you:

- what mattered
- where you were asked to endure too much
- what you will not abandon again

Anger is not the opposite of love.

It is the protector of it.

Releasing Guilt Without Erasing Meaning

Guilt often tries to keep connection alive through suffering.

As if pain were proof of devotion.

But love does not require self-punishment.

You do not dishonor what mattered by letting yourself live fully.

You honor it by carrying forward the truth it revealed.

Closing Reflection

There is nothing wrong with the emotions you haven't said out loud.

They arose for a reason.
They stayed because they needed safety.

You can offer that safety now—
without judgment, without performance.

Alchemy Pause — Closing

Before moving on, take one gentle breath.

Notice if your body feels even slightly more spacious than before.

That is enough.

Continue when you're ready.

Chapter Eight — The Loneliness Beneath the Story

Loneliness is often mistaken for the absence of people.

But the loneliness that follows loss is something deeper.

It is the feeling of being **unmet** in a world that continues
as if nothing sacred has shifted.
The sense that no one can quite reach the place you are
standing now—
not because they don't care,
but because they cannot feel what you feel from the inside.

This loneliness does not come from being alone.

It comes from being **changed**.

When Language No Longer Reaches

After loss, you may notice that words stop working the
way they used to.

You try to explain what you're experiencing, and the
explanation feels thin.

People respond kindly, generously even—
but something still feels untouched.

This can create a quiet withdrawal.

Not because you don't want connection, but because connection suddenly requires more effort than you have.

Loneliness grows in this gap—
between your inner reality and the world's ability to meet it.

The Loneliness Inside the Body

Loneliness is not just emotional.

It often lives as:

- a hollow feeling in the chest

- a tightness in the throat

- a heaviness that settles when the day goes quiet

It can appear even when you are surrounded by others.

Especially then.

This is because loneliness after grief is not about company.

It is about **attunement**.

The body longs to be recognized in its new shape.

Why Loneliness Feels So Personal

Loneliness often comes with shame.

You may think:

- *Why do I feel this way when I'm not alone?*

- *What's wrong with me that I still feel disconnected?*

- *Why can't I just rejoin life the way I used to?*

But loneliness is not a character flaw.

It is a signal that something intimate has shifted and has not yet found resonance outside of you.

Loneliness is the ache of **unshared truth**.

Meeting Loneliness Without Fixing It

Our instinct is to solve loneliness quickly.

To distract.
To socialize harder.
To fill the silence.

But loneliness does not respond to noise.

It responds to **presence**.

When you allow loneliness to exist without trying to cure it, it often softens. Not because it has been eliminated, but because it no longer has to shout to be noticed.

Loneliness becomes less about isolation
and more about listening.

Alchemy Pause — The Heart (Compassion Lens)

Pause here.

Place one hand on your heart.

Notice if there is ache, heaviness, warmth, or numbness.

Instead of asking how to make it go away,
try offering yourself this quietly:

Of course this feels lonely. Something meaningful changed.

Let the feeling be acknowledged without commentary.

Stay for a few slow breaths.

Loneliness as a Threshold

Loneliness often appears at thresholds.

Between who you were and who you are becoming.
Between what was shared and what now must be carried
internally. Between familiarity and truth.

This does not mean you will always feel this way.

It means you are in transition.

Loneliness marks the place where the old world no longer
fits and the new one has not yet fully formed.

Learning to Keep Yourself Company

One of the quiet initiations of grief is learning how to be
with yourself in ways you never had to before.

Not with distraction.
Not with self-improvement.
But with gentle companionship.

This does not replace relationship. It prepares you for
truer ones.

When you learn to sit with loneliness without abandoning
yourself, something essential happens:

You become safer to inhabit.

Closing Reflection

Loneliness does not mean you are disconnected from life.

It means life is asking you to listen more closely to yourself.

This is not exile.

It is an inward turning that precedes deeper connection.

Alchemy Pause — *Closing*

Before continuing, take one gentle breath.

Notice that even in this moment of quiet,
you are not entirely alone.

You are here—with yourself.

Continue when you're ready.

Chapter Nine — When Spiritual Bypassing Fails

For many who walk a spiritual path, grief arrives with an extra layer of confusion.

You may know the language of trust.
Of surrender.
Of impermanence.
Of love beyond form.

And yet—
here you are, undone.

This can feel like a personal contradiction.
As if grief were proof that you misunderstood something.
As if pain were a sign you have not practiced well enough.

But grief does not contradict spirituality.

It exposes where spirituality has been used to **avoid feeling**.

What Spiritual Bypassing Looks Like

Spiritual bypassing is rarely intentional.

It often sounds gentle. Reasonable. Elevated.

It says:

- *Everything happens for a reason.*

- *They're in a better place.*

- *I should be grateful.*

- *This is just my ego resisting.*

Sometimes these phrases are true.

But when used too early, they function like a lid—keeping grief contained before it has been honored.

Bypassing does not mean you lack faith.

It means your system is trying to survive by staying in the mind.

Why Bypassing Feels Necessary

Grief destabilizes identity.

Spiritual frameworks can feel like a handrail—
something familiar to hold when the ground is moving.

So the mind reaches for meaning quickly.
For transcendence.
For reassurance.

This is not failure. It is protection.

But protection becomes limitation when it prevents honest
contact with what hurts.

Truth Before Transcendence

Here is the quiet truth many discover the hard way:

You cannot transcend what you have not first **met**.

Presence must come before perspective.
Feeling before framing.
Truth before teaching.

Spirituality that cannot sit with grief becomes brittle.

Spirituality that can becomes embodied.

Grief asks you to let go of answers long enough to feel
what is true.

When Faith Gets Rewritten

Grief often dismantles inherited beliefs.

Not to leave you without faith—
but to give you a truer one.

One that is not dependent on outcomes.
One that does not require bypassing pain to stay intact.
One that allows love to coexist with devastation.

This kind of faith is quieter. It does not announce itself.
It does not rush to explain.

It stays.

Alchemy Pause — The Question (No Answer Required)

Pause here.

Ask yourself softly:

What am I using spirituality to avoid feeling right now?

Do not analyze.
Do not correct yourself.

Simply notice what the body responds to
before the mind forms a conclusion.

Stay for a few breaths.

Letting Go of the Need to Be "Above"

Many people feel subtle pressure to be spiritually composed in grief.

To rise above.
To model peace.
To prove growth.

But grief does not ask you to rise above it.

It asks you to **enter** it.

Not dramatically.
Not publicly.

But honestly.

True spirituality does not distance you from humanity.

It brings you closer to it.

What Remains When Bypassing Falls Away

When spiritual bypassing loosens its grip, something steadier emerges.

Not certainty.
Not answers.

But humility.

A willingness to not know.
A capacity to feel without collapsing.
A reverence for life as it is—unresolved, impermanent, tender.

This is not lesser spirituality.

It is deeper.

Closing Reflection

If your old beliefs feel insufficient right now,
it does not mean you have lost your way.

It means your heart is asking for truth
that can withstand reality.

Let that request be honored.

Alchemy Pause — Closing

Before moving on, take one slow breath.

Notice the simplicity of being here—
without explanation, without elevation.

Continue when you're ready.

Chapter Ten — Learning to Stay

There comes a moment in grief when escape stops working.

Distraction loses its shine.
Busyness no longer protects.
Spiritual language feels thin.

What remains is a simple, terrifying invitation:

Stay.

Not stay forever.
Not stay perfectly.
Just stay long enough to not abandon yourself.

This is the moment where grief stops being something that happens *to* you and becomes something you learn to be *with*.

Why Staying Feels So Hard

Staying feels hard because everything in you has learned to leave.

Leave discomfort.
Leave uncertainty.
Leave emotions that don't resolve quickly.

Staying can feel like you are failing to cope—
when in truth, you are learning a new form of courage.

The kind that does not require solutions.
The kind that does not demand relief.

The kind that says: *I can be here, even now.*

The Difference Between Endurance and Presence

Endurance is gritting your teeth and pushing through.

Presence is softening into what is here without collapsing into it.

Many people confuse the two.

They think staying means forcing themselves to feel everything all at once.
Or reliving the pain repeatedly.
Or drowning in emotion.

But staying is quieter than that.

It is noticing the breath.
Feeling the ground.
Letting sensation rise and fall without commentary.

Staying is not intensity.

It is **continuity**.

What Happens When You Don't Leave

When you stay—really stay—something unexpected
occurs.

The emotion changes.

Not because you willed it to.
But because emotions are meant to move when they are
not resisted.

Fear peaks and then softens.
Sadness loosens its grip.
Tears arrive and leave.

You discover that you are not the emotion.

You are the space that can hold it.

This realization does not eliminate pain.

It changes your relationship to it.

Alchemy Pause — Stay (Extended Presence)

Pause here.

Do nothing for a moment.

Notice your breath without adjusting it.
Notice the sensation of being supported.

If an emotion is present, let it be present.
If nothing is present, let that be present too.

Settle into three uninterrupted breaths.

Silently remind yourself:

I can stay with this.

Staying Builds Trust

Every time you stay with yourself instead of leaving, you build something essential.

Trust.

Not confidence.
Not certainty.

Trust that you can meet reality as it is
without fragmenting.

This trust becomes the foundation for everything that comes next—
boundaries, relationships, joy, meaning.

You cannot build a life on avoidance.

You can build one on presence.

The Quiet Power of Not Fixing

Staying does not mean you never take action.

It means action comes **after listening**.

After the body has spoken.
After the nervous system has softened.
After truth has had time to surface.

From this place, decisions are cleaner.
Boundaries are clearer.
Next steps feel less frantic.

Staying teaches discernment.

When Staying Feels Impossible

There will be days when staying feels unbearable.

On those days, staying may mean:

- one breath
- one hand on your heart
- one moment of honesty

That counts.

You do not need to master this.

You only need to practice returning.

Closing Reflection

Learning to stay is not about strength.

It is about devotion—to your inner life, to truth, to the part of you that refuses to be abandoned again.

This is where alchemy quietly completes its first turning.

Alchemy Pause — Closing

Before moving forward, take one breath
and notice that you are still here.

That matters.

Continue when you're ready.

Part III — The Alchemy

The sacred turning

Chapter Eleven — What Grief Is Actually Asking

After the fire quiets, after you've learned how to stay, a different energy begins to move.

It is subtle.
Almost shy.

Grief stops demanding attention
and starts asking questions.

Not the loud questions of *Why did this happen?*
But the quieter ones that surface when the nervous system finally feels safe enough to listen.

Grief, at this stage, is no longer only an ache.

It is a messenger.

Beyond "Why"

The question *why* keeps the mind busy but the heart distant.

Why looks backward.
Why searches for cause and logic.
Why often circles endlessly.

Grief eventually asks something else:

What now?
What matters?
What truth did this loss uncover that I can no longer ignore?

These questions do not demand immediate answers.
They ask for **attunement**.

The Requests Beneath the Pain

When listened to patiently, grief often asks for very simple things:

- more honesty
- slower living
- truer boundaries
- deeper rest
- relationships that feel safe instead of impressive

Grief strips away tolerance for what drains you.

It reveals what you were enduring quietly before the loss—misalignment, self-betrayal, over-functioning, silence.

This is not because grief makes you bitter.

It makes you **clear**.

Grief as an Initiator

In many traditions, initiations involve loss.

Not because loss is sacred in itself,
but because it removes what no longer belongs.

Grief initiates you into a deeper adulthood of the soul.

One where:

- you listen before you commit
- you feel before you explain
- you honor your body's signals
- you trust what is quiet and steady

This is not a personality change.

It is a return.

Learning the Language of Subtlety

Grief rarely shouts at this stage.

It whispers through:

- fatigue when something is off
- tension when a boundary is crossed
- heaviness when a choice is misaligned
- ease when something is true

This is the body translating wisdom.

When you learn to listen here, you no longer need crisis to tell you the truth.

Alchemy Pause — The Question (Listening Mode)

Pause here.

Ask yourself—softly, without expectation:

If my grief could speak without urgency, what would it ask of me right now?

Do not search for an answer.

Notice what arises as sensation, image, or simple knowing.

Let the question rest inside you for a few breaths.

When Answers Arrive Slowly

The mind wants clarity in paragraphs.

Grief offers clarity in fragments.

A sentence that lingers.
A realization that surfaces while walking.
A boundary that suddenly feels non-negotiable.

Trust the pace.

What is meant to guide you will repeat itself gently
until you are ready to hear it.

You Are Not Being Asked to Become Someone Else

Grief does not ask you to reinvent yourself.

It asks you to **stop abandoning what you already know**.

The truth you sense now is not new.

It is newly unavoidable.

And while honoring it may change your life,
it will feel less like effort and more like relief.

Closing Reflection

Grief is not here to take from you endlessly.

At a certain point, it begins to give back—
clarity, simplicity, integrity.

If you listen, it will show you how to live in a way that
honors what was lost without losing yourself.

Alchemy Pause — Closing

Before turning the page, take one breath.

Notice the quiet intelligence within you
that has been listening all along.

Continue when you're ready.

Chapter Twelve — Reclaiming the Parts You Left Behind

Loss does not only take something away.

It reveals what you set down along the way in order to survive.

Pieces of yourself you quieted to keep peace.
Instincts you muted to stay connected.
Desires you postponed because there wasn't room for them then.

Grief has a way of calling these parts back.

Not loudly.
Not all at once.

But persistently.

What Gets Left Behind

When life becomes overwhelming, we adapt.

We become practical.
Responsible.
Strong.

We learn which parts of ourselves are welcomed and which are inconvenient.

Often, the parts that go missing are not dramatic.

They are subtle:

- curiosity
- playfulness
- tenderness
- intuition
- the ability to rest without guilt

These parts don't disappear. They wait.

Grief loosens the grip of who you had to be and creates space for who you actually are.

Why These Parts Return Now

When something significant is lost, the psyche reassesses.

What matters?
What is no longer negotiable?
What am I no longer willing to sacrifice?

Grief lowers your tolerance for self-abandonment.

It brings back the parts of you that know how to feel deeply, choose honestly, and listen to the body without justification.

This is not regression.

It is **integration**.

The Fear of Wholeness

Reclaiming lost parts can feel strangely vulnerable.

You may worry:

- Will this make me too sensitive?
- Will I disappoint people if I change?
- Will I lose stability if I honor what I feel?

These fears are understandable.

You learned to survive by compartmentalizing.

But wholeness does not make you fragile.

It makes you coherent.

Inviting the Parts Home

Reclaiming yourself is not a dramatic ceremony.

It happens quietly.

When you pause instead of pushing.
When you say no without over-explaining.
When you let joy arise without suspicion.
When you rest without earning it.

Each small choice signals to the system: *It is safe to come back now.*

Alchemy Pause — The Body (Reconnection)

Pause here.

Bring your attention into your body.

Notice one place that feels distant, numb, or guarded.

Place a hand there gently.

You don't need to fix anything.

Just acknowledge the presence of that part—
as you would greet someone returning after a long absence.

Take three slow breaths.

Silently offer this:

You're allowed to be here again.

When Parts Begin to Respond

As you offer safety, you may notice shifts.

Not immediately.
Not dramatically.

A softening.
A sensation of warmth.
A subtle emotional release.

These are signs of trust returning.

The body responds to consistency, not force.

You Are Not Becoming Someone New

Reclaiming lost parts does not mean abandoning the life
you built.

It means bringing **more of yourself** into it.

You are not dismantling who you are.

You are completing yourself.

What returns now is not who you used to be—
but who you would have been if you had not learned to
disappear in small ways.

Closing Reflection

Every part of you that adapted was intelligent.

Every part that went quiet was protecting something.

You do not need to judge those choices.

You only need to recognize that the conditions have changed.

You are allowed to come home to yourself.

Alchemy Pause — Closing

Before continuing, take one breath
and notice the sense of space inside you.

Something is returning.

Continue when you're ready.

Chapter Thirteen — Love Without an Object

There comes a moment when you realize something surprising:

The love did not leave.

It simply stopped attaching itself to a single form.

For a long time, love felt inseparable from a person, a role, a future. It had a direction, a focus, a destination. And when that destination disappeared, love seemed to turn painful—restless, aching, homeless.

But slowly, almost imperceptibly, love begins to change its posture.

It stops reaching outward.
And begins to **radiate inward**.

When Love Detaches from Form

We are taught that love is something we give *to* someone.

But love is also something that **moves through us**.

When the object of love is gone, the energy of love does not vanish. It looks for another way to circulate. If it cannot move, it hurts. If it is allowed to move freely, it transforms.

This is the difference between attachment and love.

Attachment says, *I need you here for this to exist.*
Love says, *I exist regardless of form.*

Grief is often the passage between the two.

———

The Fear That Love Will Disappear

Many people resist this phase unconsciously.

They worry:

- If love no longer aches, does it mean it wasn't real?

- If I stop longing, am I forgetting?

- If love changes shape, am I betraying what mattered?

But love does not require suffering to stay true.

Love that matures becomes **less desperate**, not less sincere.

It softens its grip without losing its depth.

Love as a State of Being

At some point, you may notice that the qualities you
associated with loving someone—
tenderness, generosity, patience, attunement—
begin to show up elsewhere.

In how you speak to yourself.
In how you move through the world.
In how you notice beauty without needing to possess it.

This is love without an object.

Not romanticized.
Not dramatic.

But steady.

It does not need to land anywhere specific to feel real.

Alchemy Pause — The Heart (Expansion)

Pause here.

Place one hand on your heart.

Imagine the feeling of love not as something reaching outward, but as a gentle warmth spreading inward and around you.

No one needs to receive it.
Nothing needs to happen.

Let the sensation exist on its own.

Stay for a few breaths.

Silently remind yourself:

Love is allowed to live in me.

From Longing to Presence

Longing contracts the body.

Presence expands it.

As love becomes less attached to outcome, you may notice more ease in your chest, more space in your breath, more patience with uncertainty.

This does not mean you will never miss.

It means missing no longer defines the experience of loving.

Love becomes something you *are*, not something you chase.

What This Makes Possible

When love is no longer tied to a specific object, it becomes safer.

Safer to feel.
Safer to offer.
Safer to receive.

It no longer threatens to disappear if circumstances change.

This is why people who have grieved deeply often love more honestly afterward.

They are no longer bargaining with impermanence.

They are present with reality.

Closing Reflection

Love does not end when its form changes.

It becomes more spacious.

What once felt like loss begins to feel like capacity.

And you realize—quietly, without fanfare—
that the love you were afraid of losing was always yours.

Alchemy Pause — Closing

Before turning the page, take one gentle breath.

Notice the steadiness of love when it no longer needs to go anywhere.

Continue when you're ready.

Chapter Fourteen — Devotion to the Self

After love releases its grip on form, something steadier asks to take its place.

Not confidence.
Not certainty.
Devotion.

Devotion to the self is not self-improvement.
It is not self-focus.
It is not turning inward to escape relationship or responsibility.

It is the decision—made quietly, repeatedly—
to stop abandoning yourself when it matters most.

What Devotion Is (And Is Not)

Devotion is not indulgence.

It does not mean always choosing comfort.
It does not mean avoiding challenge.
It does not mean centering your preferences above all else.

Devotion means **staying aligned with your inner truth**, even when doing so costs you approval, familiarity, or ease.

It is the commitment to remain present with yourself in moments where you once would have disappeared.

―――

Why Grief Teaches This So Clearly

Loss strips away excess.

What remains is stark and honest.

You begin to notice where you have been:

- overriding your body's signals

- explaining yourself too much

- tolerating what drains you

- staying quiet to keep connection

Grief makes these patterns impossible to ignore—not to shame you, but to interrupt them.

Devotion becomes necessary because self-betrayal becomes unbearable.

―――

The Difference Between Boundaries and Walls

Devotion to the self is often confused with withdrawal.

But boundaries are not walls.

Walls keep life out.
Boundaries keep *truth* in.

A devoted relationship with yourself allows you to say:

- *This no longer feels right.*

- *I need more time.*

- *I can't carry this anymore.*

- *This matters to me.*

Without apology.
Without justification.

Devotion gives your inner life a structure strong enough to live inside.

Choosing Yourself Is Not a Rejection of Love

Many people fear that choosing themselves will make them cold, selfish, or unavailable.

But self-devotion does not reduce love.

It **clarifies** it.

When you stop abandoning yourself, you stop asking others to rescue you from that abandonment.

Relationships become cleaner.
Expectations soften.
Connection becomes mutual instead of compensatory.

Devotion restores balance.

Alchemy Pause — The Ground (Sovereignty)

Pause here.

Feel the weight of your body.

Notice the steadiness beneath you—
the floor, the chair, the earth holding you.

Let your spine lengthen slightly.

Silently offer yourself this truth:

I am allowed to stand in myself.

Stay for three breaths.

The Quiet Strength of Staying Aligned

Devotion is rarely dramatic.

It looks like:

- leaving earlier than expected

- resting when you used to push

- telling the truth before resentment builds

- choosing simplicity over approval

These moments may go unnoticed by others.

But they are deeply felt by your nervous system.

Each one reinforces safety from the inside.

Devotion as a Daily Practice

You do not become devoted to yourself once.

You practice it.

In small choices.
In pauses.
In listening before responding.
In checking whether something feels aligned—

not impressive, not expected, not familiar—
but *true*.

Devotion is consistency, not intensity.

Closing Reflection

Devotion to the self is not about becoming untouchable.

It is about becoming **inhabitable**.

A place you can live inside without shrinking, bracing, or performing.

This devotion does not isolate you.

It makes you trustworthy—to yourself first, and then to others.

Alchemy Pause — Closing

Before moving on, take one breath
and feel the steadiness of being rooted in yourself.

Nothing needs to be proven.

Continue when you're ready.

Chapter Fifteen — The Heart as a Temple

After devotion comes reverence.

Not the kind that elevates you above your humanity,
but the kind that invites you to treat your inner life
as something **worthy of care**.

The heart, after grief, is no longer naïve.
It has been cracked open, burned, softened, rebuilt.

And what remains is not fragile.

It is sacred.

From Survival to Sanctity

For much of life, the heart functions as a workhorse.

It adapts.
It endures.
It keeps loving even when conditions are unkind.

Grief interrupts this pattern.

It says: *You can no longer treat what is precious as expendable.*

When you begin to see the heart as a temple, your
orientation changes.

You stop asking how much you can tolerate.
You start asking what deserves entry.

A Temple Is Not a Fortress

A temple is not closed off.

It is open—but with intention.

Not everything is welcome.
Not everyone has access to the innermost chambers.
Not every demand deserves a response.

This is not judgment.

It is discernment.

When the heart is treated as sacred space, you become
more selective—not because you are hardened, but
because you are honoring what has been entrusted to you.

Ritual Replaces Reactivity

In a temple, nothing is rushed.

Movements are deliberate.
Transitions are marked.
Silence has meaning.

After loss, the heart begins to crave this kind of pacing.

You may notice yourself slowing conversations.
Pausing before commitments.
Listening more closely to subtle signals.

This is not hesitation.

It is respect.

Alchemy Pause — Breath + Heart

Pause here.

Place one hand on your heart.

Inhale slowly, imagining the breath moving directly into this space.

Exhale gently, as if softening the walls around it.

Do this for three breaths.

Silently offer yourself this reminder:

My heart deserves reverence.

What You Protect Shapes What You Create

When the heart becomes a temple, boundaries stop feeling like loss.

They feel like maintenance.

You protect your energy not out of fear,
but out of devotion to what you are building now.

This creates a subtle but profound shift:

You no longer give your heart away indiscriminately.
You **share** it from a place of choice.

Sacred Does Not Mean Untouched

A temple is not sterile.

It holds fire, incense, offerings, grief, joy, prayer.

Your heart will still feel.
Still break open at times.
Still love deeply.

Sacred does not mean protected from pain.

It means pain is not allowed to desecrate what is essential.

Living from Reverence

When you live from reverence, your life simplifies.

Decisions feel clearer.
Relationships feel truer.
Your inner world feels less chaotic.

You stop negotiating with what diminishes you.

You begin aligning with what honors life.

Closing Reflection

Your heart is not a battlefield.

It is not a resource to be depleted.

It is a temple—
one shaped by fire, loss, devotion, and love.

Treat it accordingly.

Alchemy Pause — Closing

Before turning the page, take one breath.

Notice the quiet dignity of being here,
inside yourself.

Continue when you're ready.

Part IV — The Gold

Living after loss—not smaller, but truer

Chapter Sixteen — Carrying Love Forward

There is a quiet fear many people carry after loss:

If I let myself live fully again, will I leave love behind?

This fear makes sense.

For a long time, grief has been the bridge that kept you connected.
Pain felt like proof that love still mattered.
Suffering felt like loyalty.

So the idea of joy—of forward motion—can feel like betrayal.

But love does not ask you to remain in grief to stay true.

It asks you to **carry it wisely**.

The Difference Between Carrying and Clinging

Clinging is holding on out of fear.

Carrying is honoring without collapse.

When you cling, love feels heavy, anxious, fragile.
When you carry, love feels integrated—
woven into who you are rather than strapped to your back.

Carrying love forward does not mean revisiting the past
constantly. It means allowing what mattered to inform
how you live now.

Love as Continuity, Not Attachment

Love does not disappear when its original form ends. It
becomes continuity.

It shows up in:

- the way you listen more deeply
- the way you choose honesty over comfort
- the way you protect what is tender
- the way you recognize what truly matters

This is love matured by loss. Not louder.
Not dramatic. But steady.

When Memory Softens

At some point, memories begin to change temperature.

They may still bring tears, but they also bring warmth.

This is not forgetting.

It is integration.

Memory becomes something you can touch without being pulled under.

And when that happens, love no longer feels like something you must *manage*.

It becomes something that accompanies you.

Alchemy Pause — The Heart (Gentle Carrying)

Pause here.

Place one hand on your heart.

Imagine love as something you are carrying *with* you—
not ahead of you,
not behind you,
but beside you.

Notice how that feels in the body.

Stay for three breaths.

Silently remind yourself:

I am allowed to live and still love.

Joy Does Not Erase Meaning

Many people believe joy will diminish what mattered.

But joy does not erase love.

It **expresses** it.

Living well becomes an act of remembrance.
Choosing presence becomes a form of devotion.
Allowing pleasure becomes a way of honoring life itself.

You do not honor love by shrinking.

You honor it by becoming more alive.

Letting Love Travel Light

As you move forward, love may no longer need to be
heavy to be real.

It may show up quietly—
in moments of gratitude,
in tenderness toward yourself,
in compassion for others walking their own thresholds.

This is love that knows how to travel light.

Closing Reflection

You do not need to choose between remembering and living.

You are allowed to do both.

Love carried forward does not anchor you to the past.

It steadies you in the present.

Alchemy Pause — Closing

Before continuing, take one gentle breath.

Notice how love feels when it is allowed to walk beside you.

Continue when you're ready.

Chapter Seventeen — Boundaries as Sacred Containers

After loss, boundaries stop being theoretical.

They become **necessary**.

Not because you are fragile,
but because you have learned—viscerally—
what happens when what is precious is left unprotected.

Grief sharpens discernment.

You no longer ask, *Can I handle this?*
You begin to ask, *Should I?*

Why Boundaries Change After Loss

Loss strips away tolerance for what drains you.

Things you once endured quietly—
over-explaining, emotional labor, misalignment, rushed connection—
begin to feel unbearable.

This is not bitterness.

It is clarity.

Grief teaches you that energy is finite, presence is sacred, and your nervous system deserves consideration.

Boundaries arise naturally when self-respect replaces survival.

Boundaries Are Not Punishment

Many people associate boundaries with rejection.

But boundaries are not walls meant to keep others out.

They are **containers** that allow connection to happen safely.

A boundary says:

- *This is where I end.*

- *This is what I can offer.*

- *This is what I need to remain present.*

Without boundaries, love leaks.
With them, love stabilizes.

The Body Sets the Boundary First

Before the mind knows a boundary is needed, the body signals it.

A tightening in the chest.
A sinking feeling in the gut.
A sudden fatigue around certain people or conversations.

These signals are not inconveniences.

They are intelligence.

When you honor bodily signals early, you don't need dramatic boundaries later.

———

Alchemy Pause — The Body (Yes / No Awareness)

Pause here.

Bring your attention to your body.

Think of something or someone currently in your life.

Notice what happens inside:
Does the body soften—or brace?

You don't need to judge the response.

Just notice.

Take three slow breaths.

Silently remind yourself:

My body tells the truth before my mind catches up.

Clean Boundaries Feel Quiet

Healthy boundaries do not require justification.

They are not reactive.
They are not dramatic.

They sound like:

- *I need more time.*

- *That doesn't work for me.*

- *I'm not available for that.*

- *This is as far as I can go.*

Spoken calmly.
Held consistently.

If a boundary feels shaky,
it often means it is being negotiated internally.

Devotion strengthens boundaries from the inside out.

Boundaries Create Safer Love

When boundaries are clear, relationships relax.

Resentment decreases.
Expectations become visible.
Connection feels mutual instead of extractive.

You stop giving from depletion and start sharing from steadiness.

This is not withdrawal.

It is maturity.

Closing Reflection

Boundaries do not make you less loving.

They make love **possible**.

They protect the heart not from life, but from erosion.

What you protect is what you can sustain.

Alchemy Pause — Closing

Before turning the page, take one breath.

Notice the relief that comes
from honoring your limits.

Continue when you're ready.

Chapter Eighteen — Relationships After Awakening

After grief, relationships feel different.

Not because you have become distant, but because you have become **aware**.

What once passed unnoticed now registers clearly— tone, pacing, emotional availability, respect for boundaries.

You are no longer relating from survival or longing.

You are relating from **presence**.

Why Some Relationships Fall Away

Awakening does not make you superior.

It makes you **honest**.

And honesty can disrupt relationships that were built on:

- over-giving
- unspoken expectations
- shared avoidance
- roles that required you to stay small

As you stop abandoning yourself, some dynamics lose their glue.

This can feel like another loss.

But it is not rejection.

It is realignment.

From Attachment to Attunement

Before grief, connection may have been driven by attachment:
Who needs me?
Who chooses me?
Who makes me feel safe or wanted?

After grief, connection is guided by attunement:
Can we be present together?

Is there mutual respect for pace and truth?
Does this relationship support wholeness?

Attunement feels quieter than attachment—
but far more nourishing.

The End of Over-Explaining

One of the first changes people notice is a reduced need to explain themselves.

You stop justifying your feelings.
You stop narrating your boundaries.
You stop managing others' reactions.

Not because you don't care—
but because you trust yourself enough to let your truth stand on its own.

This is not withdrawal.

It is grounded self-respect.

Alchemy Pause — The Question (Relational Lens)

Pause here.

Think of a current relationship.

Ask yourself gently:

Do I feel more myself here—or less?

Notice the body's response before the mind answers.

Take three slow breaths.

Let the information land without action.

Meeting Others Where They Are

Awakening also brings compassion.

You begin to see that others are doing the best they can with the tools they have.

You may love people who cannot meet you where you are now.

This does not require cutting them off.

It requires **clarity**.

You can hold care without over-functioning.
You can stay kind without staying silent.
You can step back without closing your heart.

New Relationships Feel Different

Relationships formed after grief often feel simpler.

There is less urgency.
Less performance.
More listening.

Connection grows at the speed of trust, not intensity.

These relationships may not look impressive from the outside.

But they feel **safe**.

When Intimacy Becomes Possible Again

True intimacy after grief is not about merging.

It is about meeting—
two whole people, present and honest.

You no longer seek to be completed.

You seek to be **seen**.

And you allow others the dignity of being seen as they are,
not as you need them to be.

Closing Reflection

Relationships after awakening are not about perfection.

They are about presence.

You no longer bond over avoidance or fantasy.

You connect through truth.

That is quieter.

And infinitely more sustainable.

Alchemy Pause — Closing

Before continuing, take one breath.

Notice the steadiness of connection
when it is no longer driven by fear.

Continue when you're ready.

Chapter Nineteen — Joy Without Betrayal

Joy returns quietly.

Not as fireworks.
Not as certainty.
But as small, almost suspicious moments—
a laugh that escapes,
a body that relaxes without warning,
a morning that feels lighter than expected.

And with it often comes a sharp, reflexive thought:

Is this allowed?

Why Joy Can Feel Like a Threat

After loss, joy can feel disloyal.

Grief has been the language of devotion for so long that anything softer feels like abandonment.

You may worry:

- If I feel joy, does it mean I didn't love enough?
- If I enjoy this moment, am I forgetting?
- If I move forward, am I leaving something sacred behind?

These fears are understandable.

Grief taught you how much love mattered. Joy now asks you to trust that love does not require suffering to remain true.

The False Choice We're Given

Many people believe they must choose:

Grief **or** joy.
Memory **or** presence.
Loyalty **or** aliveness.

But this is a false dichotomy.

Joy does not erase grief.
It **coexists** with it.

The heart is capable of holding sorrow and delight at the same time. It always has been.

What changes is permission.

Joy as a Capacity, Not a Reward

Joy after loss is not a prize you earn for surviving.

It is a capacity that returns when the nervous system feels safe enough to receive.

This joy is quieter than before.
More grounded.
Less demanding.

It does not insist that everything is okay.

It simply says: *Life is still here.*

And that is enough.

Alchemy Pause — The Breath (Receiving)

Pause here.

Take a slow inhale through your nose.

As you exhale, soften the chest and belly.

On the next inhale, imagine allowing in just **five percent more ease**—
no more than that.

Exhale gently.

Stay for three breaths.

Silently remind yourself:

Receiving does not erase what mattered.

Letting Joy Arrive in Pieces

Joy does not return all at once.

It arrives in fragments.

A song you can listen to again.
A flavor that tastes vivid.
A conversation that feels nourishing.

When you allow these moments without immediately
questioning them, joy learns it is safe to stay.

Joy leaves when interrogated.
It settles when welcomed.

Honoring Love Through Living

There is a deeper truth beneath the fear of betrayal:

Living well is not a denial of love.
It is an **expression** of it.

Love that shaped you did not intend for you to remain
suspended in pain.

It intended to make you more alive.

When you allow joy, you carry love forward—
not as weight, but as vitality.

When Joy Triggers Grief

Sometimes joy will unexpectedly open grief again.

A beautiful moment reminds you of what is gone.

This does not mean joy was a mistake.

It means your heart is integrated enough
to feel the full spectrum at once.

Let the tears come if they do.
Let the laughter remain if it wants to.

Nothing needs to be corrected.

Closing Reflection

You are allowed to experience joy without proving
anything.

Joy is not a verdict on your grief.

It is life continuing to offer itself to you—
gently, patiently, without demand.

Alchemy Pause — Closing

Before turning the page, take one breath.

Notice any trace of ease in your body—
even the smallest amount.

That is not betrayal.

That is healing.

Continue when you're ready.

Chapter Twenty — Becoming a Safe Place for Yourself

At the end of grief, something unexpected remains.

Not answers.
Not certainty.
But **safety**.

Not the kind that promises nothing will ever hurt again—
but the kind that trusts you will not disappear when it
does.

This is what the journey has been preparing you for all
along.

The Safety You Were Seeking

In the beginning, safety may have felt external.

A person.
A future.
A role.
A sense of control.

Loss shattered those structures.

But what emerged, slowly and quietly, was something more reliable.

A relationship with yourself that does not require perfection, certainty, or performance.

You learned how to stay.
How to listen.
How to honor your body and your truth.
How to carry love without collapsing.

Safety became internal.

———

What It Means to Be Your Own Refuge

Becoming a safe place for yourself does not mean you no longer need others.

It means you no longer **abandon yourself** to keep connection.

You pause when something feels off.
You listen when the body speaks.
You tell the truth before resentment builds.
You rest without justification.

You trust your inner signals even when the outer world is
loud. This is not isolation. It is sovereignty.

The End of Urgency

One of the clearest signs of healing
is the absence of urgency.

You no longer rush to resolve discomfort.
You no longer panic when emotions arise.
You no longer need to explain yourself into safety.

You know how to be here.

And that knowing changes everything.

Alchemy Pause — Closing Integration

Pause here.

Place one hand on your heart
and one somewhere grounding.

Feel the steadiness of your breath.
The presence of your body.

Silently remind yourself:

I am a safe place to land.

Stay for a few breaths.

Let the truth of that statement settle.

What You Carry Forward

You do not leave grief behind.

You carry forward:

- clarity instead of confusion
- devotion instead of self-betrayal
- presence instead of urgency
- love without attachment

You carry forward a deeper intimacy with life.

This is not an ending.

It is a foundation.

When Grief Visits Again

Grief may return—
in new forms, new losses, new thresholds.

But it will not meet you the same way.

Because now, it will find someone home.

You.

Closing Reflection

You were never meant to bypass grief.

You were meant to be shaped by it—
not into someone hardened,
but into someone **inhabitable**.

A place where love can rest.
Where pain can pass through.
Where joy is allowed to return.

You are not what you lost.

You are what remained
and learned how to stay.

Final Alchemy Pause

Take one final breath.

Notice the quiet completeness of this moment.

Nothing needs to be added.
Nothing needs to be fixed.

You are here.

And that is the gold.

Closing Blessing — The Gold You Carry

May you remember, when grief returns in quiet waves or sudden tides, that you have already learned how to stay.

May you trust the body that carried you through what the mind could not solve.
May you listen when it whispers, and rest when it asks.

May love move through you freely now—
not clutched, not withheld, but honored in its many forms:
memory, presence, tenderness, joy.

May you release the belief
that suffering is the cost of devotion.
May you know that living fully is not a betrayal of what mattered, but a continuation of it.

May your boundaries be clear and kind.
May your heart remain open and protected.
May your life be shaped not by urgency, but by truth.

And when the world feels uncertain again, may you remember this:

You are not lost.
You are not broken.
You are not behind.

You are the gold that remained after the fire—
softened, clarified, and capable of holding life as it is.

May you walk forward gently.
May you rest when needed.
May you trust what you have become.

And may you always know
that you are a safe place to return to.